A Bunch of Heather

An Anthology

Glimpses of life... the glad, the sad, and the mad!

By

Heather Blackwell

Copyright © 2024 by – Heather Blackwell – All Rights Reserved.

It is not legal to reproduce, duplicate, or transmit any part of this document in either electronic means or printed format. Recording of this publication is strictly prohibited.

Table of Contents

Dedication i
About the Author ii
The Climb 1
A Prayer 2
Coming Home 3
January Morning 4
Glory to God 5
Coming Home from Grasmere 6
May Time 7
The Farm 8
Ashfield Lake 9
Southport Beach 10
Prayer of a Twentieth Century Sheep 11
I am a Creator God 12
Day After a Death 13
Freedom 14
Free as a Bird 15
The Butterfly 16
The Breath of God 17
Mind Games 18
In times of darkness… 20
Picking up the Pieces 21
Love Has Many Faces 23
The Angel Top 24
Bisky 25
Knitting… 26
The Jug 28
Memories of Kirby Lonsdale… February 2012 29
The Dance 30
Night after Night… 31
Gary's Visit 34

Letter from Bethany	36
Mary's Reflections	38
He called me by name	41
Calvary Remembered	44
Judas	46
While Shepherds Watched…	48
Rush Hour	49
On Preston Station	50
Mum's Hairdo	52
The Birthday Party	54
The Diet	57
Day Care	59
The Fish Pie	62
Sunday Sailor	65
The Bonfire	68
Shekinah	69
Something heard…	70
Finally	71

Dedication

For Ken, the beloved.

About the Author

Married to Ken and with 3 tolerant adult children, Heather has supported her husband in pastoral ministry and has worked for 25 years in Community Health.

Heather has volunteered in a hospital, a prison, and with Sleepstop, a charity supporting homeless young people.

She has led writing workshops and has contributed to Pause for Thought on local radio.

Heather was born in the South of England and now lives in easy reach of the Lake District.

Her passions are the countryside, needlefelting and Radio 3.

Now retired and with 3 grandsons, she enjoys the funny side of family life with Teddy, an effervescent Cockapoo.

Proceeds from this book will be donated to impoverished brick kiln workers of Dohlan Hithar, a village in S. Pakistan.

The Climb

It is not comfort we are promised;
The colour-coded ambience of computer culture.
Our only right is the green of the earth,
The blue of the sky
And all the myriad variations of creation's theme.

It is not safety we are promised.
No freedom from shock or sudden fear,
Or pain.
It is not companionship we can be sure of…
Except HIS, the Eternal Friend.

We are not cloistered from grief, distress,
Bereavement. Loss.
All these are ours, at one time or another,
And He is ours also;
The Eternal Guide—urging us up the rock face,
Persuading us on, giving us joy,
With the wind in our faces, the sun in our eyes,
And the tears flowing.

It is not safety we are promised,
But the wounds of an active life,
And He with us.
Tending our hurts,
Preparing the cleft,
Leading us higher
To the summit,
Where one day, we shall see the view,
We shall see HIS face,
And we shall be satisfied.

A Prayer

Lord God, I thank You that You are other than myself.
I thank You that You are not limited by my emotions,
Whether faith or fear.
I thank You that you cannot be manipulated by my pleading
Or shaped by my tears.
I thank You that You do not reflect my character
But You want me to reflect Yours.
I thank you that You work by all means
In all ways, at all times
And that You do wonders in the earth beyond my imaginings.
I thank You that You mine gold, emeralds and opals
Out of the solid rock
And that those things which I pronounce invincible,
Are as clay in Your mighty hands.
I thank You that You do not despise my weakness and my waverings
But You cause me to look up, away from my own uncertainties,
Towards Your steadfastness.
I thank You that You challenge me
With the strength of Your compassion,
To move on, even when my heart and my flesh fail me.
I thank You that You are the Truth forever.
I thank You that You are not shrunken to my needs
But that You gloriously outshine them.
I thank You that I am not nothing,
But that You are teaching me
That You are Everything.

Coming Home

It would be easier for me, Lord, if You would shout at me
And bring me screaming into Your kingdom.
If You would wield authority and a big stick.
Why, I would weaken and skulk into Your realm,
Defeated by sheer force and weight of words.
But You don't shout at me.
You hold out bloodstained hands and say, quite simply, "Come"
And I can take it or leave it. Or leave it.
If I come though, Lord, I have to put down a few things.
I have to say, "Not my will, but Yours"
That's what You said, didn't You, before the cross?

You had a choice. You made it willingly, not easily.
Your Father didn't force You to the cross.
He didn't MAKE you die.
You didn't have to go that way.
And yet, You did.

You gave your cheek for the fatal kiss,
Your back for the lash,
Your head for the thorns
Your hands for the nails,
Your feet for the hammer's blow.
Freely…freely….

So, if I am to follow You, it must be freely.
Not grudgingly or miserly, but with a generous heart.
Lord, help me not to drag my feet, weighed down by my agenda.
Help me to run to You, through caution to the winds,
And come with empty hands to Calvary,
To be reborn.

January Morning

Wonderful January morning.
Sky soaring
Bird wheeling
Sun blinding
White scudding
Amazing.

Clean cutting
Wet shining
Blue skimming
Highflying
Lung bursting
Fantastic
January morning!

Drink it…
Great gulps of white frosted
Translucent
Tongue tingling
Wonder.
Taste it!
Feel it!
Live forever!

NB: Early for work in Southport, I paused in Morrison's car park. It was such a special morning. I scribbled my thoughts on the paper bag from my breakfast bun.

Glory to God

Glory to God for Springtime things
For ladybirds with spotted wings
For fledglings thriving in the nest
For May tree in her lacy best.

Glory to God for clear blue sky
For silver birches reaching high
For dancing catkins on the trees
For pollen drifting with the breeze.

Glory to God for misty dawn
For diamonds glistening on the thorn
For apple buds and daffodils
For purple haze on distant hills.

Glory to God for new bluebells
For burdened bees in waxen cells
For celandines in emerald grass
For spiders busy with their task.

Glory to God for life and light
For sense and sound and gift of sight
For bursting happiness that sings
In gratitude for Springtime things.

For this inheritance is mine
From God, my Father, the Divine,
Bright promise of a world to come
When all Creation shall be one.

Coming Home from Grasmere

Sky rose purple
Skilful brushstrokes
Painting evening
Spilling gold into the gathering dusk
Like some bright promise
Of eternity.

Snow filmed mountains
Tinged with pink
Glittering waters
With a band of gold
Dividing light from shadow
Bright from dark.

Behind the jagged hills
A glorious Carnival,
With big brass band
Bold bellowing bassoon
A vivid jangling orchestration
Giving way to simple strings
And then….
Night falls.

May Time

Beyond the open window, the good red wine,
familiar company, the buzz of conversation,
gnats swarm in pale sunbeams.
Clematis scrambles pink.
New bluebells spike the ragged flags;
Forget me not.

Beyond the gate and fed by recent rains,
the river swiftly snakes.
The air is still.
Cream candles light the chestnut where
the blackbird sings.
May blossom scent clings close.
Green misting willows light the further bank.
Above them, primary colours fill the arcing blue.
Fire gas roars red.
Majestically, the balloon soars.
Lord of our landscape.

A kingfisher skims by.
Slowly, dusk falls.

St Ebbes: Oxford.

The Farm

Sun rises amber in a rose gold sky.
The corded fields are ribbed and rimed with frost.
Bright rubies glow on emerald-spangled boughs.
A pheasant skitters in the glittering grass.

Quicksilver slicks the ancient puddled yard.
Hens squawk and squabble in the rotting shed.
The cockerel crows; the farm awakes. Day breaks.
Smoke breath of cattle mists the hawthorn hedge.

The farmhand, yawning, stoops to set Sam free,
As the old collie strains his rusty chain,
With lolling tongue and eager questing nose,
Busy he goes, t'inspect his royal domain.

Ashfield Lake

Do swans still celebrate the sun
And do blue dragonflies for fun
In vivid ecstasy gyrate
On shimmering Ashfield Lake?

Do diamonds glisten on the web
And are full fish still being fed
With artful bait, early and late,
On misty Ashfield Lake?

And did we find the rainbows end,
My joyous, best remembered friend,
Or did the sun sweet magic make?
Enchanted Ashfield Lake.

Memories of young adventures with a dog called Rover..

Southport Beach

Lord, when I set off half cocked, unready, hurried,
my day remains like that, accelerating powerfully to overtake
and drawing closer to the next man's bumper....
Chafing at traffic lights whose slow command
I cannot overrule or override.
Lord, on those days I achieve little but excuses,
lots of them, throughout the day,
punctuating my relationships with breathless explanations
of my lateness, inefficiency ,
or both.

Today, the rush of yesterday has caught me up.
I cannot find my instruments.
I search for them, by phone.
Of course, I'd brought them home. Or had I?
Cheerfully, the girl confirms that I had left them at the Rest Home,
twenty miles away.
I altered my arrangements for the day
and listened to You Lord,
on the way here at fifty miles an hour,
unhurried, Lord, for me.

So now I'm watching as the tide at Southport
covers the wide sands as quickly as a trotting horse.
A moment since, there was a sweep of gold
and now it's vanished under grey sea water.
Help me to cherish all my days,
to treat the present moment carefully,
lest suddenly, the tide comes in unnoticed
drowning the past and present
and sweeping me into the future,
unprepared.

NB: The diary of the self employed can be chaotic. As a Chiropodist both in surgery and with a domiciliary work load, things sometimes went awry!

Prayer of a Twentieth Century Sheep

Lord, I would be fed, not simply filofaxed.
Lord, I would be pastored, not merely processed.
Lord, I would be prayed with, not only photographed.
And I would be led, so that I can follow,
With less of the circular route.

Lord, I crave for fellowship along the way.
Something more than a simultaneous bleating
in the section labelled "worship".
Lord, my longing is for something more than a preordained minute
under "Miscellaneous "
or even a prayerfully prepared verse from the Ansaphone.

Lord, I'd like reality.
Deliver me from organised religion
Release me, if You please.
Speak to me Lord
in ways that I can understand.

What's that Lord? Did You speak?
You rang me up one day?
And left a message?
After the tone… of course…
I could not fit You in for weeks?
Because my book was full?
Oh surely not! I'm truly sorry Lord!
And yes… I get the message…
What a blessing I have had a cancellation…
Will next Tuesday do?

NB: We can all be disappointed at times with our experience of pastoral care and Church life. However, I have had to be reminded that nothing can take the place of time with God. Our fellowship is first of all with the Father, and with His Son, Jesus Christ. I need to make time for that relationship, first of all.
At the time of writing I was busy as a self employed Chiropodist with a full diary.

I am a Creator God

I am a Creator God
I make all things new.
Where there is destruction,
I will rebuild:
Where there is tearing up,
I will replant.

Trust Me in the darkness
that leads to Springtime.
Lean hard on Me in the time
that leads to Harvest.
I am a faithful God:
I keep my promises.

My mercy reaches to the highest Heavens.
My faithfulness beyond the furthest clouds.
I am a Creator God.
I make all things new.
Lean hard on Me:
Trust me in darkness.
and you shall find me faithful.

Day After a Death

Daybreak brings in new bird shell sky,
Thin gold leaf flutterings,
Slim crimson wands, frost rimmed.
Gnarled mossy fingers, copper splashed,
Beseeching Winter.

Such rustling, darting, dipping…
A flash of scarlet breast and earth brown wings.
Such scurrying and making merry…
A flick of a grey brush around a silver trunk.
Such shining eyes, such bulging furry cheeks.
Such fun!

Vivid haws and holly berries,
Jewel bright glitterings.
Frost encrusted emeralds, with gold and trembling rubies.
Wisps of sapphire wood smoke
Curling, rising, breathing Autumn,
Bright celebration of the rest of death
Before new life.

And I, should I today be sad,
scuffling the remnants of a season past?
Or should I not instead be glad that he,
his outworn body left at last,
Savours eternity with Christ, his Friend,
And shares a glory which will never end?

Freedom

Unfurl your vivid banner in my life , dear Lord,
And let me dance for You
In jewelled colours.
May my Winter turn to Spring
And glorious Summertime,
And may I raise the ruby glass of your new wine
To my parched lips
And taste new life.
At last.

NB: Dancing with banners was an unknown joy… When at last I took courage and waved my turquoise banner among the bluebells at Ellel Grange, the experience was wonderfully liberating.

Free as a Bird

You opened the door of my cage
and a little brown bird flew out:
She'd been darting about in her limited space,
pecking and peeking, all of a flutter,
and now she is free.

But ringing her bell for attention,
is a bright budgerigar:
A colourful bird with flashes of white
and an unusual streak in her tail.
She sways on her perch and examines her face in the glass.
She speaks a few words to herself, then hops to the door
and balances there, sensing her freedom
but not understanding it yet.

The brown bird is free; I thought she was me
but I am the budgerigar too.
I never knew; until now.
They showed me the ways of a little brown bird,
but I am the budgerigar.
I have learned how to speak, and I'm tired of the glass.
Give me others to talk to, with meaning.

You have opened the door…
Who shut me in there?
It was "they", long ago,
But now if I stay,
It is ME!
I WILL fly!
Show me how to be free,
Free as a bird.
Show me now!
Show me how to be ME!

NB: Claustrophobic limitations can be placed on us by well meaning authoritarian figures, often during childhood. The concept of freedom can come as a revelation to us and entering into it can be a deliciously terrifying adventure….

The Butterfly

Here I am,
Beating my wings on the glass
Smooth shining barrier between me and my freedom.
I shall never get out
I shall never break free
I shall never escape.

Outside there is greenness,
Blue sky, distant sea.
Everything beckons,
Calls and entices,
But I am excluded.
The world dances on,
Without me.

It takes me so long to discover
The window is open.
The way to my freedom is there…
Has been there
All the time.
I was so busy, beating my wings ,
Exhausting myself at the glass,
I forgot to look up
But now, I am free.

Outside in the air, I am dizzy with joy!
Where to go? What to see? Who to be?
For now there are choices and I must be brave to decide.
Back there, behind glass, I was wanting so much
To be free.
And now that I have it, I need so much courage
Just to be ME.

The Breath of God

I see a butterfly in the distance,
A bright scrap of silk, fluttering in the wind.
She is going from flower to flower,
sipping and tasting, enjoying her freedom.

A hand is stretched out.
The butterfly settles there.
She spreads out her wings.
They shimmer with gold dust.

A finger reaches out.
"Don't touch my wings" she says.
"It makes them transparent…
I can't fly."

There is a pause while the finger is withdrawn.
"Just breathe on me", says the butterfly, softly.
"Just breathe on me."

The butterfly is resting now,
cupped in protective hands.
She may fly another day.
She is free to do so:
She is willing.
But now, wings stretched out to the sun,
she is resting ,
and she feels the breath of God on her wings.

NB: Inner healing takes time and the tenderness of God. We can intervene too soon in fragile lives….God is at work, gently leading us to Jesus.

Mind Games

Struggling for form, for substance
Rising and falling in some hazy underworld,
Fragments of truth beckon
But elude my grasp.

I am forever seeking solid ground.
Forever reaching out to dim perceived realities
And grasping
Nothing.
Forever weary in the search
Pursuing misty goals which circle nearer
Then recede again leaving me
Empty.

"We all feel like that sometimes. "
Do we?
Poor doomed beings.
"You'll feel better soon"
Oh yes, I know.
The sight and scent of daffodils,
Cream roses climbing russet walls,
Enamelled buttercups in emerald grass,
Windsong and scent of sea spray.
All these sustain me,
Hold me in trembling hope
Above the pit
Like some stray butterfly.

Where are the everlasting arms?
Is there no voice to whisper comfort in the dark?
Just silence and the slimy pit.
The waters overflow…
I know they cannot.
But they do.

What do I seek?
Security?
As frail and fragile as the spiders web
Which stretches on the thorn?
And happiness?
As frail and lovely as new bird shell.

"Oh, pull yourself together"…..
What self?
And what togetherness?
Bright splinters of my childhood
Turn in kaleidoscope unceasingly.
They will not come together.

I must go home.
Where is my home?
I am displaced…
I am alone.

Or am I?
Fleetingly, I sense that with me
In this void
Is He who made me.
I am known by Him.
I am loved.
I am forgiven…
And I may yet reach home.

NB: Undiagnosed and untreated depression is unspeakably isolating.
Thankfully the memory of it is in the past and I am grateful for the help and empathy I have received.
Beauty is dazzling when we leave the darkness behind.

In times of darkness…

In times of darkness, that which is most important
are not our thoughts about ourselves or about God;
These only reflect our inner distress, confusion and turmoil.
Our thoughts at such times are a reflection of our own human weakness
and are not to be received as TRUTH.
The only Truth is to be found in God: In his character and in His Word.
What is important, are HIS thoughts about us.
"How precious are Your thoughts to me O God.
When I awake I am still with You"

Do not rely on your own thoughts to affirm Truth;
The disciples despaired;
The empty tomb, the resurrected Lord, proclaimed the ultimate Truth,
That Jesus is alive, that His Word is true, and that, regardless of our feelings,
He will never leave us or forsake.

Psalm 139

Picking up the Pieces

Lord, sometimes I feel I can't take anymore of pain
Or shame, or sickening disappointment.
Someone said, who didn't know,
"Your big balloon has burst."
Balloons are cheap, synthetic things.
They tug on fragile strings,
High in the sky, primary colours,
Red, blue, and shouting yellow.
Basic and a little vulgar.
Big bold balloons ,bursting with an ugly bang
And childish tears and anger.

Yes.. I suppose it has.
Burst, I mean.
My personal balloon.

And yet, the colours that we had were beautiful.
Sky and sea coloured; spring and autumn,
Bright like summer, yet with winter's shadows menacing.
Sometimes muted, sometimes dazzling,
All the changing patterns of the seasons mingled
In the jigsaw of our lives, seeming to make a picture.
It looked complete, just fleetingly, and we were glad and grateful.
A savage jolt displaced it all. Deliberately.
And now it lies fragmented on the floor,
A broken, worthless thing.
Or is it?
We can stoop and try most painfully again
To piece it altogether.
It will take time, but it is possible, and given grace and strength,
Which has not failed us yet,
We can take up the fragments of our lives
And make it all again, slowly and carefully,
With faith and hope and love;
The things which last.
Once a balloon has burst,

That's it.
Torn tattered remnants, sticky with stale breath
Lie in the dirt. A broken toy. Forever.
But all the colours of our jigsaw still remain, though scattered now
And with God's help and by His living breath
We'll make it all again
Without a trace of bitterness.
Please God.

NB: Loss of any kind is universal but always devastating and takes time to process. With faith and hope and love and the help of God, it is possible to rebuild, but the picture will always be different. I wrote this after listening to someone else's pain and reflecting on my own.

Love Has Many Faces

Love has many faces.
You may glimpse them in the flames of a well lit fire,
The mug of tea on a rain soaked night,
The locking or unlocking of a door.
You may glimpse it in an anxious look,
An unwanted enquiry; a brief touch as you turn away

Love has many faces.
You may see it in the curl of breakfast bacon,
A random text at an unwonted hour.
You may see it in a stubborn wisp of shining hair
Or in the calloused hand that grips the wheel,
A rigid focus on the task as yet undone.

Love has many faces.
You may see it in the silent weariness of early morning
Or in the red rimmed eyes of a long day.
You may see it in the hunched back at the computer screen,
The bending to some routine task,
The turning smile reserved for you.
You will see it in the practised faithfulness whatever the weather.
That is LOVE.

"Sorry", "please" and "thank you" are the words of love, well spoken,
And at the last, "Forgive me. I did not understand."

NB: Gratitude rarely comes naturally. We must learn it. It is a language of love.

The Angel Top

There it is again
Wrapped in creased tissue
A white angel top.
Drawing my eyes and my fingers
Touching my memory.
It is lacy and small.
I hold it up close to my cheek;
Faint smell of lotion and talc,
Silky soft.
The long sleeves have stretched.
Washed in a hurry by hand
In whatever I'd got.

I hung it outside in the sun
With nappies and baby gro's
Small frilly things
Catching the sun
With the buzzing of bees
And the whisper of wind
In the leaves.

The first day she wore it,
I buttoned it up at the front.
Well, I didn't know any better.
Three cute pearly buttons.
She lay in the sun and sucked at her toes
Til a neighbour came by and pointed it out.
"You've buttoned that baby up wrong!"

These days she wears Levi's and brief cotton tops
That cling close.
She smells of Givenchy and paints her ten toenails
Dark blue.
She's out and about and says "Cool!"
To whatever I say.
So I keep it, the white angel top.
It still makes me smile, now and then.

Bisky

From day one, you made your mark:
Bat eared, a cavernous mouth,
Kneading your way to my heart.

You were an independent cat,
Not given to listening or obeying rules.
"Not there" we said repeatedly.
You did it anyway, working out by day and night,
Treating our home as your very own personal gymnasium.

Outside, you were fearless
Confronting larger, ancient, wiser cats,
Playing leapfrog, skidding,
Leaping for butterflies,
Investigating bugs and bees.
Only backing off when stung.

You followed us to work, to school, to church
And to the bus stop. Noisily.
Excluded from the car,
You sat upon the roof, paw trailed on the screen.
When we relented, you curled up on the driver's lap
Or stretched on the back shelf,
Contentedly.

That last evening,
You luxuriated in my chair
Head on the arm, tail twitching,
Dreaming safe dreams.
Next day, the milkman found you
Broken in the road.
A careless joyful cat,
Our Bisky.

NB: Bisky, our tortoiseshell kitten, followed Dorcas, Miranda, and Benjy in our cat family. She was greatly loved, but without road sense, meeting her demise after a very happy year.

Knitting…

Untangling the wool of my life is a slow process;
My fingers seem all thumbs and though I sometimes think
I've glimpsed the end
It vanishes again as my searching fingers part the strands.

I wish I had been knitting from the first
Instead of playing with the wool and wishing for another colour.
At least by now, I'd have a garment of some size
Instead of all this mess.

Sometimes, I want to throw it all away;
Begin again.
I want to cut the threads with jabbing movements of the scissors.
But then I would have so many different ends,
False ones, misleading trails…
There's no short cut to usefulness
Or joy.

Oh Lord, I'm sorry.
I got me in this mess.
Refused the age old way of doing knitting;
Refused the patient repetition,
The casting on, the casting off,
The picking up of those lost stitches;
The increasing and decreasing.

When we show our garments at the end,
Will my tangled ball of wool be there
Discarded on the floor?
Or will You, the great Teacher, come alongside patiently,
And help me to cast on again?
Please find the thread for me before the class is over.
Please cancel my rebellion.

NB: There is a lot to be said for careful listening and observance of conventional wisdom.

Fortunately, for those of us who try to take short cuts, there is forgiveness, redemption and the opportunity of a new beginning. Sadly, I am still a poor knitter.

The Jug

The jug of terracotta clay
Cost fifty pence.
'Twas large and shapely and looked well upon my window sill
Filled with the corn and poppies that those days were fashionable.
But when I filled the jug with water from the tap
It leaked, and rivulets ran from the crack across its width.
The jug was flawed.
So now I fill my jug with water just below the line
And still the poppies bloom, just briefly,
And the corn gleams gold.

Sometimes , I feel a bit like that old jug….
I know I look quite well, until I'm put to use,
And then the flaw appears.
But I'm still useful for some work.
One day, the flaw will be made whole
And healed most wonderfully.
But while I'm waiting for that time,
I'll be content with water just below that line
And flowers will bloom in spite of it
And make somebody glad.

NB: Our limitations are not always obvious to others but we ourselves are very aware of them. I have had to come to terms with my own and choose to flourish in spite of them.

Memories of Kirby Lonsdale… February 2012

A long low barn, a broad oak door,
Fire logs stacked and fir cones making
Molten lava…
Deep armchairs.

Smell of toast and breakfast chocolate
Leathered chestnuts, spitting logs.
Hissing kettle, clink of mugs…
The smoke alarm.
A birthday cake..
(A camper van)

Jigsaws, lego, playmobile,
Pounce and Rummikub.
Uno, laughter, friendship, hugs,
Pastels, crayons, watercolour.

Low grey cloud and felting fog
Fine rain falling.
Scoured lanes and ripped raw hedges
Lumped mud. Quagmire.
Spreading pools and seething becks
Boundaries liquifying.
Mossed green tree trunks.
Rank rottenness.

The lesser spotted woodpecker….
A long tailed tit.
Snowdrops nestling in bright mosses.
An early daffodil.
A gold leaf boat
Whirling downstream.

And YOU
With ME
FOREVER.

The Dance

Rwanda; 2010

The drumming began softly, almost imperceptibly, like the first drops of rain before the storm.
The patter became a stream which swelled into a torrent as the drumbeat filled the simple place.
A ripple swept the room as on grass in a dry wind. Bare feet shifted on sand; Eager hands clapped to the rhythm. Butterfly colours fluttered together: oranges, reds, blues and greens. Colours of Africa. Hips swayed, bodies bowed. Broad smiles lit brown faces. The air thrilled to the sound of their singing.
The source of the beat was a rusty oil drum, a goatskin stretched taut across its mouth. Beside it, a glossy child, perhaps seven years old, tapped expertly with palms and fingers, his feet keeping time with his hands; his huge eyes watchful; his round face inscrutable.
A toddler rocked to and fro on her heels, her face a dark centre in a ragged blossom of pink taffeta. Older children leapt, clean limbed and agile, arcing and twisting in sinuous celebration.
Withered grandparents swayed to the beat, graceful yet yearning, with learned humility, until we too, succumbed to the magic . We took their proffered hands in joyous friendship and joined the dance with them.

NB: This was a memorable evening when we visited Kibogora Hospital, Rwanda, for the second time with medical friends.

Night after Night…

Silently,
Skeletal black shadows drag themselves across our living rooms
On plastic screens,
Night after night.

We feast our eyes unwillingly
On suffering of such degree
We turn away, ashamed of witnessing
This holocaust.
The flies which buzz around the children's mouths
We long to brush away with gentle hands.
Our arms would cradle tiny forms
And ease the melting bones of grandmother's
With wrinkled flesh like withered leaves
In a dry wind.

We would draw water from our filtered taps
And make the desert bloom again.
If we could bring to birth the young green shoots
By shedding all our tears upon dry sand,
This we would do.

But now, the scene has changed
And wounded refugees lie helpless on the ground
Before our eyes.
Beseeching brothers make us gaze on their distress.
Our sisters weep in silent agony.
The little children die in front of us
In bloodied coats and anoraks
Bought in the local store.

The guns and shells supplied by nations
Struggling with their personal deaths
Explode in fire,
Singling out victims in a mindless anarchy.
The bloodier scenes are locked away

In journalistic archives.
What we see is sanitised and censored
For the News at Ten
Thanks be to God.

And where is He?
In our mute helplessness we look for Him
Who put the stars in space
And caused the sun to shine
And rain to fall.
He who called children to His knee
And promised millstones to the one
Who stumbled them.
Whose are those millstones now?
Ours hang about our necks
Night after night,
And we would ourselves of them,
But money will not buy our peace.
We pay the price, but still the world is shrieking,
Dying nightly in our homes,
At ten pm.

And what of Waco?
As the fireball stains the sky
And seventeen children die alone
Without the help of us
Or anyone,
What can we say?

This modern day Messiah, David Koresh,
Did not save but crucified his followers,
One by one.
Just like the News at Ten
At suppertime,
Night after night.

We drink the bitter dregs of our nightcap
And slowly climb the stairs
To haunted sleep,

Uncomforted by news of the warm front
Expected on the North west coast tomorrow.

The help we seek is from our God
Who paid the price and shed His blood
For us, and for the BBC.
He rose again exultantly
To show us that this time and space
Is not the end.
For though the plastic screen may seem
The limit of our world tonight,
The limit of our sight is not this life….
One day we'll understand it all
As simply as a little child.
We'll stand outside of time and find forgiveness,
And forgive the One we did not comprehend
But now see face to face.
Until that day, we'll gather
At the shrine erected by the BBC
And shed our tears
For all our sakes.

NB: The news was terrible that year…Malawi, Kosovo, Waco…
I wrote this in a desperate response and with agonising questions…

Gary's Visit

The tiles on the vast floor are grey.
The walls are cream and pockmarked,
Pitted with pathetic history.
The stacking tables are set out,
Grey melamine with metal legs.
The chairs are standard issue by the Home Office,
In regulation blue.
Such calming colours.

At every table sits a man,
A lean grey man, dressed like his fellows,
With cropped bristly hair.
The air is grey with curling rings of stifling smoke,
Exhaled by thin lips creasing sallow faces.
At every table is a visitor or two.
Between them, plastic cups containing
Greyish liquid, wet and warm.
A woman sits and sips, her small pale eyes
Staring past her man's left shoulder,
Her face expressionless.
The man looks blankly past her, silently,
His fingers drumming on the wipe clean melamine.
They sit together but a world apart.

Children sprawl on rubber mats,
Pushing yellow trains and building drunken towers
Of scarlet bricks.
The towers fall. The trains collide.
The children nag each other,
Pointing, pulling, pushing, pinching.
An adult remonstrates; a truce is called,
Unwillingly, uneasily, eyes darting covert looks
At the grey watchers at the tables,
Childishly aware that they provide the entertainment
For the afternoon; that every move of theirs
Is focus for slight conversation,

Punctuated by short puffs and sips ,
And tapping fingers.

Two prison officers preside indifferently,
Their fingers playing with their keys,
The telephone in reach.
A great clock ticks the time away.
A small boy leaves the safety of the mat,
To stand beside his father, quietly.

The woman and the man remain engrossed,
His fingers fumbling awkwardly
Inside her leather coat,
Their faces curtained by her flowing hair,
And she half sitting on his knee.
Timidly, the child puts out his hand,
And touches her himself.
Not looking down, she says,
"Gary, ger off, ger out of 'ere."
He turns, and walks away unsteadily,
Back to the rubber mat and plastic toys.

Then suddenly, a bell shrills and the dead awake.
There is a buzz of purposeful activity.
Chairs are scraped back, the empty cups collected,
The dog ends crushed to blackened stubs.
The visit over, Gary's mother touches him at last,
And with a little shake, takes him away.

NB: For a time, I volunteered at Wymott Prison, looking after children at visiting time. It was a revelation in so many ways….

Letter from Bethany

Dear Judith,

I must write and tell you what's been happening in Bethany since I was last in touch. It's always been so quiet here until Jesus turned up. I've told you about Him…you'll remember He brought Lazarus to life, my friend Martha's brother? What a day that was ! It certainly put Bethany on the map! Anyway, Jesus came to supper at Simons' who lives next door to me…the one who was a leper?... But that's another story. To cut it short, Jesus made him better so now he has a social life and things are different for him now, very different.

So, he asks Jesus to supper, and he says to me;

"Anna, will you help with the cooking and serving? " That's never been his strong point since his wife died. So I said "Yes!" and I was really excited! I just love being around Jesus. And when He's talking… SUCH talk…..I could listen to Him forever.

I cooked a good bit of fish, fresh from the lake, just as the Master likes it. Martha gave me a tip or two. The bread was fresh baked, and what with the grapes, the figs, the olives and the sparkling wine, the table looked well in the lamplight..

The house was crowded by the time Simon's friends had arrived; not that he has many mind, on account of the leprosy and all, but some of Jesus' disciples came too. That Judas was there Judith, the dark one….I can't take to him somehow, I don't know why.

Anyway, the meal was going well and little Tabitha was helping me out. She;s ten now, my youngest but you know that….We stood in the shadows waiting in case we were needed. Such laughter there was and such noisy talk…That's men when they get together ! But with Jesus, there's a quietness as though He's at peace with Himself and He doesn't need to impress anyone. He noticed us too and was friendly like, to Tabitha and me. So we stood watching….

Suddenly, such a commotion. Mary from the corner house comes in, Martha's sister. Not invited! She pushes past Tabitha and makes straight for Jesus who was still eating ,mind. The room went so quiet. She's a strange one that Mary. She has had a bad name around here…a bit of a one with the men: But we thought she was through with all that. She's quietened down a lot lately and it's Jesus who has helped her. She thinks the world of Him. It's common knowledge.

Anyway, quick as a flash ,she'd taken the stopper from the flask she was clutching, and without a word, pours it over Jesus' head and Him still eating! We all knew what it was from the sweet smell of it. It was nard and it must have cost a fortune! Left over from Lazarus' burial most likely. Well! Everyone was dumbstruck… all this stuff trickling down Jesus' face and onto his clothes, the floor. The perfume was overpowering and nearly half a pint of it. Mary never does things by halves!

That Judas spoke first and his face was like thunder:

"Who let HER in? " he growled. "Think of the price of that nard, how many poor could have been fed! The woman's crazy! Who let her in?" He was glaring at me and Tabitha started to cry. Simon was all red faced and blustering. He was so embarrassed see with all Mary's sobbing and crying and her letting her hair down as well…. You should have seen her Judith!

Jesus was wiping His face, then He touched Mary on the shoulder. "Let her alone," He said. "She has done a very beautiful thing. One day she will be known for it all over the world. She has anointed me ahead of my burial.".

Well, that shut everyone up. A burial ? What could He have meant ? Mary crouched at Jesus' feet, hugging Him to her and crying still. I wished I'd had her courage then, and her generosity, because Jesus loved her for it; I wished I'd had something more to give than plain fish and bread and olives. But when it was over and Mary had gone, more lamps were lit and more wine was poured then Jesus caught my eye. He just spread His hands wide and laughed, that deep warm laugh He has, and I laughed too.

"Thank you, Anna " He said. "Thank you." We laughed together at the scene Mary had made; the disturbance she'd caused through her love, and the outrage and the recklessness of it all. And I knew that I loved Him too, but differently and that it was enough; He accepted my offering too. He accepted ME. He loved ME, just the same.

I must go now , Judith….there is more bread to bake….but I wanted you to know all this and be glad for me. Come to Bethany when you can, and see for yourself!

Shalom …

Your friend Anna

Mary's Reflections

It was late in the day when we came to Bethlehem,
And I knew every bony crevice of the donkey's back
Which jolted under me all the long way from home.
Home held the crib made lovingly by Joseph
Within the crib were garments waiting for our first born son.
We knew we waited for a son, the angel told us so,
Firstly to me and then to Joseph.

We'd thought we were an ordinary pair,
In love, and waiting for the wedding.
That night, upon the donkey's heaving back,
I wished that it were so.
I wished the baby had been ours, made in our love together
And that our families waited joyfully for our return
And for the birth.

As the pains came close and strong, the donkey fell behind
The straggling line of travellers.
I urged him to go on; I sensed that time was short.
My Joseph asked at every place but they were all full up
For everyone had come before us.
I remembered that the angel said I must not be afraid.
If this child were God's Son, then surely he would keep us safe.

Soon there was comfort in the straw as I lay down,
A lamp upon the beams, illuminating cobwebs
And the cows as they munched hay and snickered softly
In the shadows.
At last, the baby came quite easily into the stable world,
A tiny frail Messiah, drawing new breath and wailing weakly
In the cold night air.
I think I wept at first, before joy came. Maybe because of weariness
But even more, because I felt the loss of Him immediately.
I knew he was not mine, this child, this firstborn one.
I knew He was the world's, God's little Christ, born to redeem.
Yet, curling close, He looked like any other child, except perhaps,

More dear, more beautiful than any other.
None could deny, in spite of everything,
I was His mother.

That seems a long, long while ago,
Thirty three years long,
Since that coldness and the manger,
And the singing starlight and the shepherds
Crowding the small space.
We shared an agony together all those years ago
And I was bound to Him and He to me
With cords of love which spanned infinity.

Today, we shared another agony.
I watched Him die a savage death, nailed to a cross,
A rough wood cross, the wood he used to carve with Joseph,
Back at home.
No angels there that I could see,
No wise men came today to help me understand
The whys and wherefores of this dreadful day.
No starlight shone for Him, but thunder groaned and lightning spoke,
And there was darkness mourning Him and silencing the shrieking chaos,
And the jeers of enemies.

"Father forgive them…" Simple words, but hard to utter on a cross
When every breath was pain.
Simpler to slip away in silence.
No. He finished all He came to do.
I know that now….
I saw Him change the water into wine.
I saw him give a man His sight and cause another man go running home
For the first time.
I've known Him touch a little girl and give her life, instead of death,
And turn her parent's pain to joy and gratitude.
I've seen him quiet at prayer, drawing fresh strength from God Himself
To give Himself again to those that needed Him.
An ordinary man, my son, with homely skills and a man's love of life,
But sin, forgiveness, steadfast love, were things He spoke of with authority
Like God, Himself.

Oh, if I never see His face again and if I never hear Him speak my name,
I know that he is God, Messiah, with the power to rule creation,
Change a nation, melt a heart, and turn a stone to flesh.
I know I see a little part of God's amazing plan for me
And for the world He made.
I know that Jesus has a Saviour's heart.
I'm thankful I could play some hidden part
In claiming back the world from Satan's grip.

So now, I wait, to see what God will do.
To see if blood, sweat, tears, the cross, the tomb, mark out the end.
And yet, within my heart, this sudden surge of hope,
That death cannot contain this son of mine,
Who is not mine,
But God's.

Oh, He may not have been my own and yet there is this certain bond,
If He may not belong to me, I certainly belong to Him!
God cannot die!
And so I wait, in faith and hope, to see the promises fulfilled,
And death become a vanquished foe,
For Him, for me, for you.

He called me by name

It was early, too early for birdsong, as I went on my way.
The night had been long and tearwashed for me,
A thousand thoughts pressed on my mind,
Grisly scenes from the Friday before.
What a day it had been, out there on the hill,
With thunderclouds looming most of the day.
The moaning of men taking a long time to die.
The laughter and shrieking of those on a day trip,
A trip of a life time, at the place they call
Calvary.

I stood at the foot of the cross
And held its' rough wood in my hands.
He was out of my reach. I could not touch Him now,
But I knew that He knew up there on the cross,
If I could have done more, then I would.

He looked for His mother. She was standing with me
And His words were for her—I was glad.
She'd had very little, right from the start
Yet she shared what she had with her son.
She watched Him live life she scarce understood
Then die this hard death, which shamed her
And wounded her heart.
He gave her to John—that's how it should be,
For he cared for her more than the rest.

We stood at His feet. We could do nothing more,
Not even give Him a drink. The soldier did that.
Put a sponge on the end of a spear.
But though He was thirsty, He would not give in.
Not a drop would He take; nothing more.
At last He cried out "IT IS FINISHED!"
And there in the darkness we held one another
And shuddered, in grief and relief.
At least it was done; the pain and the groaning,

Those great sobbing breaths that tore at Him so.
They were gone. He was dead. He was free.

Now, after the wood, they have sealed Him in stone
And I'm on my way to Him now.
It is finished for Him, but not finished for me.
Somehow my life must go on.
Maybe in the silence of this early morning,
I'll find strength from somewhere or someone?
I don't know.
I only know that I need to be near Him,
With my Lord, whether living or dead.
Noone can stop me.
It's for women to weep over those that they love…
To weep at the birth and to weep at the death…
It's our right. None can take it away.

But there's nobody there! The soldiers are gone!
Now that's strange, they were guarding Him well…
And that mighty great stone, they have rolled it away!
And the tomb! It is empty! Oh no!
Where shall I go and what shall I do
If I never can see Him again?
There was never a time or a place for "Goodbye"
And somehow, it needs to be said.

I'll run and tell Peter and John that He's gone
And the guard they left watching,
They've disappeared too…
Oh where shall I go and what shall I do
Without Him, my Master, my friend?

It was then that I saw Him.
I could never have guessed in the whole of my life,
That a dead man could live and could speak.
I looked at Him and He turned to me.
"Where is Jesus?" I sobbed, "Where's He gone?"
He was quiet without words for a moment,
Then looking at me, face to face, He said "Mary…"

I knew it was Him! No one ever said "Mary" like that
As if I mattered most in the world at that moment in time.
Just "Mary"---"Mary" He said.

It is JESUS!
He's risen. Come back from the dead…
The tomb…it is empty, the soldiers are gone!
He told me to tell you. He's gone on ahead.
If you go to the City… you'll find Him,
He's there!
Oh, I maybe a woman, I know, but it's true.
I knew it was He. He knew it was I.
"Mary," He said ."Rabboni!" I answered.
It's true! Jesus lives!
And He called me by name.
He's ALIVE!

Calvary Remembered

Oh it was hard to see His majesty so vulnerable.
To hear the mob yell, "Crucify!" was more than we could bear,
And yet, he had to bear much more than we.,
His was the pain, the pitting of sword points upon raw flesh.
His feet trod cobbles unprotected, bruised and bloodied
In the humid heat of that dark day.
His was the loneliness.
His was the thud of nails, the anguished cry.
Ours was the watching and the guiltiness,
Ours was the fear.
Ours was the outrage and the questionings
That scourged the mind.

Who was He now?
Who had he thought He was?
Who were we now?
The losers once again?
Deceived and the deceivers?
Back to square one?

Oh, it was hard to see this man so vulnerable,
And yet, He had to bear much more than we.
Stench of horse flesh, close hustling of harness,
Quick snapping and snarling, the pack at His heels.
Wailing of women, cursing of men,
Palm branches thrusting, in mockery now.
The crushing of bone, bone against wood,
Straining of muscle, ripping of flesh.
His was the brokenness.
Ours was the wonder that ever such horror should come upon Him.

Forgiveness personified,
Love everlasting,
Submissive in suffering,
Weak in His power.
Humanity broken and Deity glorified,

With thorns , blood and nails,
And a rough wooden cross.

His was no worthless sacrifice and He no common man.
If we were losers, we had lost before,
But not this Man.
He always kept His word and met our needs.
He knew our thoughts before we uttered them.
No loser He.
But hanging there upon the cross,
He looked as if the sum of all our losses
Held Him there.

Oh, it was hard to see His Majesty so vulnerable,
And yet, we understood that Sabbath day,
Seeing the empty tomb and later on
Our resurrected Lord,
We knew it had to be and we were glad for our sakes,
That it was this way.

NB: The disciples were thrown into emotional and mental chaos on that Good Friday. What had it all meant? What were they left with? I have tried to empathise with them and also allude to the impact of the resurrection of Jesus, the Messiah.

Judas

Judas: If only he had settled down.
Always an eye on the main chance had Judas.
Always a scheme up his sleeve.
Depending on his own efforts
Was too straight forward for him.
Riding on the back of another's success
Was more in his line.

He'd been curious.
Curious about Jesus of Nazareth.
He'd tagged along with him for three years,
Watching, absorbing, calculating.
A shrewd lad, Judas, though I say it myself.
He kept the communal purse in the end,
A trustworthy task.

He was known as a disciple of Jesus
Bur I was his mother.
I hoped, but I could not trust.
I saw him weigh and scheme
I saw him measure love and loyalty,
Cost out its' value
And toss it on one side.

MY son, my son…
Thirty silver coins they paid you
For that fatal kiss
Which clinched your grisly bargain.
And yet, you struggled with your heart within.
Took your own life,
Spilled your own blood in rage and guilt,
Despair.

I cannot guess what emptiness engulfed you
As you grasped those paltry coins.
Did you sense you'd thrown away again
The only lasting thing in life?
Pure love.

I loved you Judas with a mother's love.
Twas not enough to keep you straight
And true and clean.
You wanted it, you tested it
But it was never quite enough.
I love you still, my son
Forever.

NB: We often speak of Mary, the mother of Jesus, but spare a thought for the mother of Judas. She has her story too, and we can only imagine the pain of it.

While Shepherds Watched...

Huddled round a fire
Rough men, working for a pittance
Watching sheep, sharing stories.
Night watchmen
Men forgotten.

Then YOU God,
You sent angels with trumpets
An iridescent choir
Shimmering the midnight sky…

Awe and amazement followed fear,
Then came obedience.
They ran like men demented,
Flock abandoned,
Ran, until their own strength spent,
They knelt,
Ragged and unclean, astounded,
Before the minute Maker of the universe,
And there in that small space
They worshiped the Messiah.

YOU God
Sent angels with trumpets
And a glittering choir
To give forgotten men
A glimpse of glory
And the greatest news:
THE CHRIST IS BORN!
EMMANUEL!
God IS with us.

NB: There's no biblical evidence for trumpets… but who knows?!

Rush Hour

When silver Tubes slide into town
And business men are bearing down
On suburb stations all around
Then early morning sounds abound.
Kate is brushing Sara's hair
Lionel's calling, "Are you there?
I wish you'd hurry, darling Kate,
I hate to be late for the ten to eight!

When Sara's toilette is complete
Then Kate slips in the driving seat.
"Oh , it's tonight we're due to meet
The Jenkinsons from Jermyn Street.
Bye bye Lionel, see you soon…
I'll be lunching out at noon.
Remember darling, we've a date…
I hope you're not late for the ten to eight!"

"Come on old boy, you've cut it fine
The train's held up along the line.
You've just a sec to get the Times
The shares are up at Bentley Hines…
Hurry! I can see it coming!
Here comes Henry, he's been running!
Awfully glad you've made it mate...
It's fractionally late for the ten to eight…"

NB: Whilst a student, flat sharing in posh Pinner, I travelled by Tube to Baker Street each day, as did a host of City businessmen; think bowler hat, rolled umbrella and the necessary newspaper!

On Preston Station

PING PONG! ATTENTION PLEASE!
The train on Platform Four
Is not the train you should be on,
That went some time before.
The trains are running early
Or are they running late?
This is because the later train
Met a most dreadful fate.
A passenger, in ecstasy,
Jumped down upon the line
And danced a naked war dance;
The train *had* run to time
But this deflected it of course
And caused severe delay,
So now your train has come and gone
And you have missed your way.

PING PONG! ATTENTION PLEASE!
Please disregard that message,
I don't know what I said!
The early trains and later trains
Are muddled in my head.
I think I'll have just one more drink
And struggle home to bed.
ALL PASSENGERS! ATTENTION PLEASE!
The signal's stuck at red….

The early trains are running late,
The later trains have stopped
And frankly, speaking through this mike,
The things an awful botch.
PING PONG ! PING PONG!
I shouldn't have said that.
The problem is "LEAVES ON THE LINE"
That's the official rap.
But on the quiet, the truth will out,

A tea lady went up the spout,
And caused a stew,
Just as the train was leaving Crewe.

PING PONG! PING PONG!
Forget that I said that.
Leaves upon the blooming line!
Disrupted services!
So there!

NB: I wrote this cautionary tale whilst waiting for a long overdue train.

Mum's Hairdo

Our mum went to the hairdresser
To get a permanent wave.
She came out looking beautiful,
The style was all the rage
But when she came to wash it,
It stuck out like a bush…
She wept and sulked and hid herself
And kicked up such a fuss.

Our dad came home to get his tea
And found her in a mood.
"Whatever shrub you look like, dear,
We have to have our food!
Can't you just wet it from the tap
To flatten it a bit?"
At this she threw a pan at him
And had a screaming fit.

The atmosphere was heavy,
All through our evening meal,
When suddenly our Susan,
Who cannot stand stewed eel,
Threw all the contents of her plate
Upon the kitchen floor.
You could have heard a pin drop!
We couldn't eat no more…

"Send Susan for the floorcloth mum,"
We all cried out in chorus.
"She did the deed, the silly dweeb,"
But dad looked like a walrus,
And dashing up to get the mop,
He seized our mother's head,
"If you don't want to be a bush
Then be a mop instead!"

It did our mum a power of good.
Now she's for Women's Rights.
A woman can't be called a mop
A bush, or just a fright…
It's contrary to section three
Of Women's Liberties.
We're careful how we treat our mum.
She wears a wig now, see?

The Birthday Party

Our Jasmine had a party,
It was her birthday see,
And she invited all class four,
Except for Anne Marie;
We had her here the year before,
But she bit all the boys.
She's bigger now., with quite a bite.
We can forgo that joy!

Our Jasmine wore her frilly dress
And she looked very sweet.
It was too short, but never mind,
We like to see her feet.
We tied her hair up in some rags,
She slept in them all night.
It took her hours to get them out,
We'd tied her up so tight.

I tried to make a birthday cake.
It isn't quite my thing!
I whisked it up, just like it said,
But didn't grease the tin.
So when I came to turn it out,
I hit it with a hammer.
Is shot across the kitchen floor,
In the most frightening manner.

I gathered up the little crumbs.
And stuck it up with treacle.
If I could ice it beautifully,
I might deceive the people.
I used a lot of colouring
To get the icing pink.
Unfortunately it turned blood red.
What would our Jasmine think?

I got it right eventually.

And poured it on the cake.
It ran onto the kitchen floor
And formed a little lake.
It was just then our cat stalked in
And thought he'd try a bit.
The icing set around his paws.
The poor thing had a fit!

I tried to disengage the cat
And free its' sticky paws.
I pulled its tail hard as I could.
It seized me in its jaws.
The creature gave me such a shock
I fell into the icing
The Dad came in; "I must say dear
You don't look too enticing…

Why are you sat down with the cat
In all that stickiness?
It's nearly time for guests to arrive.
You look a shocking mess.
I'll show you how to make a cake
You just jump in the shower.
And kindly take that cat with you.
Now tell me. Where's the flour?"

When Cat and I emerged at last
There was a lovely smell
Of birthday cake baking.
And he'd iced it as well.
Not pink this time, but frothy white
And stuck the candles in.
"No one will know 'bout t'other cake.
I've stuffed it in the bin.!"

Our Jasmine was so thrilled with cake.,
She thought her dad a wizard!

She had a little taste of it
It settled in her gizzard!
She coughed and rolled her eyes and said:
"Take this to Anne Marie!
Can be her prize for biting boys…
You give it her for tea!"

We thought her so ungrateful
To scorn her birthday cake
But when we'd tried a little piece
We saw the sad mistake.
In saving time, our dad had iced
The cake with shaving foam!
Now Jasmines' little birthday guests
Have all gone spluttering home!

The Diet

Chocolate cookies are no good
For waistline or for figure
And when consumed in quantity
They cause us to get bigger.
Flavoured crisps are similar,
They make saliva flow.
One packet is not quite enough
And so we grow and grow…

We try to train our tastebuds
To yearn for finer things
But apples, pears and cucumber
Don't that same pleasure bring.
And so at last to Fatwatchers
Our heavy steps we turn
To tread the scales and pay our fee
Our habits to unlearn.

One ounce of fibre cereal
One ounce of cottage cheese
One slimline yoghurt or four plums
Our appetites appease.
We drink our own tapwater now
As if it were champagne
We gorge ourselves on lettuces
Our goal weight to attain.

We pour our slimline tonics
After our walk or swim
Our weekly treat, a muesli bar,
Our passion, to get thin.
Our partner is most anxious
We should not lose our shape.
He loves the bits we hope to lose…
He thinks that we look great!

That's cos his memory is poor.
He soon forgot that scene
When gliding down the aisle in white
We wore a size fourteen.
He loves us just the way we are
He's loyal and so staunch
But oh my dear, truth must be told,
He has a modest paunch.

So off to Fatwatchers we go,
To tread those boards together
Our one desire to lose some weight
Come wind or wave or weather.
When snuggled up on winter's nights
Our tummies rumble loudly
But we can count each other's ribs
We tell each other proudly.

But one sad day, no lettuce leaf
Has power to appease us,
We pool our money, blow the lot
On peanuts and Maltesers.
Fresh cream meringue and Yorkshire pudds,
Roast spuds and carrot cake
Black Forest gateau, fish and chips
Cause bathroom scales to quake.

We've found another diet now,
It's called: "Eat what you Like"
So just for now, we'll follow that,
And if again we run to fat,
There's always Fatwatchers,
So there!

NB: This was obviously pre decimalisation or simply to help the rhyme!

Day Care

The green team are in charge today
Of all your tender care
We'll show you where the toilets are
And where to comb your hair.
Now, can you give us your full name?
Just for the record… please.

We'll need a little specimen
If you could just oblige.
Just take this egg box into there
And leave it on the side.
Now, can I check your number dear?
Just for the record… please.

Shortage of funding sometimes means
That tapes are rather rare,
To fasten nighties at the back…
That's why dear, yours aren't there !
Can I just check your next of kin?
Just for the record… please.

We need to see how much you weigh,
Just for the anaesthetic…
A little shot for a big girl
Would be a bit pathetic.
Now, can you give your date of birth?
Just for the record… please.

We'll hitch you up to this machine
To measure your B.P.
If by mischance it doesn't work,
We'll test you manually.
Now, can you give us your address?
Just for the record… please.

You haven't had a drink have you?

Just when you brushed your teeth?
No naughty lagers on the side?
Well, that's a great relief!
Do you still know your date of birth?
Just for the record… please.

Pop on the bed now if you like.
You haven't a top sheet
You get them if you stay the night.
Sheets are for the elite!
Now do you know why you are here?
Just for the record… please.

You've come here for a horrorscope
And just a little scrape.
Mr Thing is very good.
He seldom makes mistakes.
Is there a number we could phone?
Just for the record… please?

Can you tell me your religion?
I'll just put Methodist.
Some people like to see a priest
To lay their fears to rest.
Can you spell Methodist for me?
Just for the record… see?

Cyril is coming for you now.
He'll stay behind the curtain
Whilst you get on the trolley dear,
So privacy is certain.
Can I just check your pulse for you?
Just for the record…please.

We'll give you just a little prick
To send you off to sleep.
Now here it comes… just count to ten
STOP! Hold it there Nurse Heap!
Can I just check how much you weigh?

Just for the record… please.

It's over dear.
You've had it now.
Your horrorscope is done.
Now, when you'd like a cup of tea,
Just press your bell for one.
If we're not busy taking notes
We'll hurry to your side.
You'll understand if we're delayed?
We're really rather tied.
We'd like you OUT by 5 o'clock
If you are feeling well…
Your husband may have tried to ring…
We thought we heard the bell
But we were busy taking notes
Just for the record…
See?
Now Heather, just before you go,
You know what you've had done?
And are you sure what you've to do
When you get to your home?
Are you quite compos mentis dear?
Just for the record… please.

Is this truly your next of kin?
Please show him section four.
Make sure he knows what not to do'
Just you lay down the law!
Goodbye! You'll know your full address.
It's on your records…
See?"

The Fish Pie

Mrs Elisabeth Allen
Carried considerable weight
In the W.I., the local Church
And of course, at the Annual Fete.

Because of her heavy commitments,
She decided to learn how to drive.
The car that she chose must be robust,
On account of her stature—and size.

When she told her good husband the plan,
He consulted the man at the Garage.
They considered at length, and decided for strength
On a reinforced steel undercarriage.

The car, when it came, was enormous
And painted a pillar box red.
On top of the roof it sported a turret,
For fashion, the garageman said.

The news of this new acquisition
Spread round the small town like wildfire:
Outside in the road, where the vehicle was parked,
A crowd gathered round to admire.

The neighbours all helped her get in it
Though she landed a little askew
The windscreen was small but she never complained
But cried "I've a wonderful view!"

Next morning, the brave Mrs Allan
Climbed into her new driving seat.
Twas a sign for the rest of the townsfolk
To pull into the side of the street.

Though she only intended to practise,

The monster set off with a roar.
It demolished a small roundabout,
Heading straight for the General Store.

Everyone scattered in panic
As the brute ploughed its' way through the town,
While Elisabeth Allan's poor husband
Distractedly jumped up and down.

The town was already for Britain in Bloom:
The place looked a picture throughout,
But sad to relate, when the red tank rolled through,
It took all the flowerbeds out.

Avoiding the queue at the General Store,
More by good luck than good judgement,
The beast made its' way to the Fishmongers shop
And settled itself on the pavement.

Mrs Elisabeth Allan
Emerged with her hair all awry
She strove for composure and entered the shop
Saying faintly, "I'll have a fish pie"

As the fishmonger wrapped up the pie,
The poor lady whispered her thanks.
A policeman burst in, and said with a grin,
"Mrs Allan, you'll drive no more tanks"!

"It's only a car with a turret,"
Said her husband, perspiring and mad.
"My wife didn't mean to cause such a scene.
She's even forgotten her bag"!

The fish pie was paid for with somebody's change
While the tank was towed out of the road,
Mrs Allan departing by taxi
Was delivered to her own abode.

"I never did order a tank, dear",
Blustered her husband at lunch.
"I'm terribly sorry you've had such a fright,
But listen here, I have a hunch…."

Mrs Elisabeth Allan,
Carries considerable weight
In the W.I, the local Church
And very much more at the Fete.

Mrs Elisabeth Allan
Has made a most generous donation
First prize of a Tank at the annual Fete.
It's a wonderful gift to the Nation!

Noone will ever remind her
Of the day when they all rushed to see
Mrs A drive a tank down the High Street ,
To get a fish pie for her tea…

Sunday Sailor

I thought I'd like to learn to sail
Before I got to fifty.
Apart from the odd bunion,
I still felt pretty nifty.

I borrowed books on sailing
From the local library
And started learning all the words
I'd need to sail the sea.

I memorised starboard and port
And learned to shout "Lee ho!"
I recognised the bow and stern
And thought I'd have a go.

We travelled up to Windermere,
It was a glorious day
I couldn't wait to test my skills
And sail upon my way.

But first, Bob showed us all the ropes
And introduced the tiller.
He taught us how to push and pull
He said "Now't could be simpler…

Just grasp the helm and face the sail
And hold the mainsheet steady.
When changing tack, just dodge the boom,
Now sailors, are you ready?"

I flung myself upon my craft
And sailed off all alone,
I kept my eye on distant bank,
And all my thoughts on home.

What would they do without me

If I should not come back?
The rocks were rushing at me,
I really should change tack!

I pushed and pulled with all my might
And dodged that horrid boom,
I loosed the mainsail, turned about,
Transferred my weight to soon.

I tilted slightly to starboard
Then saw my feet above me.
Before I knew it, I was in
And calling those who loved me.

"Help me, Ken!" I shouted out,
Then foolishly remembered
That he was safely sat in Church
With all the other members…

"Oh Lord, I'm very sorry
That I have sailed on Sunday'
If by mischance I come again
It will be on a Monday!"

At this appeared a rescue boat
And very worried faces
Who all leaned out and hauled me in
By my elastic braces.

I tried again, soon after lunch
I knew I could survive
'Twas just a case of balancing
And trying not to jibe.

I was set fair in sailing
When all at once a boat
Shot past my bows and caused a swell
I scarcely stayed afloat.

Then suddenly I panicked…
What was I doing here?
I should be safe and warm at home
And not on Windermere.

What if a speedboat hit me
And sank me without trace?
How would they do their ironing
And would they still say grace?

Who would pack up their sandwiches
And who would feed the cat?
Who would pick up the scattered socks,
And who would shake the mat?

I turned a little circle
And drifted out of sight
I foundered on a rocky shore,
No one had seen my plight.

After a full five minutes,
I hitched up to a rock
And stealthily climbed up the bank
And went to find dry socks.

They never found my body
Although they searched the lake.
'Twas kind of them to bother
But I was just a fake.

I never was a sailor.
I really shouldn't roam
Until new fancies take me
I shall stay moored at home.

NB: Loosely based on fact, this is an account of a memorable attempt at sailing when on an ill advised trip with a school…. Alas, so different from my brief experience of a catamaran in the Mediterranean!

The Bonfire

Do not be like children who sit around a bonfire
admiring the flames and   the coloured sparks as they fly upward.
They sit with their backs to the darkness and only move into the shadows
when the fire gets too hot.
Children warm their hands at the bonfire and chatter among themselves.
I would have you take a torch from the fire and confront the darkness .
My light will overcome the darkness.
But the darkness will remain while you huddle round the fire.
You must take my light out.

Why do you flatter your hearts?
I have told you these things in many different ways.
Obedience must not stop with the mind.
Obedience must be active.
Better to leave the bonfire and to run ahead of the coming volcano
Whose lava will touch every street.

NB: This came to me as I enjoyed a bonfire on November 5th 1993. Matthew 25 was on my mind. It was about this time I began to volunteer at Wymott Prison some Sundays, and we opened our home for Sleepstop, a Barnardo scheme for young people made suddenly homeless.

Shekinah

We have felt the scorching fire of God as He has roared through the valley of our lives; touching the things which are precious to us; turning to ashes the things we considered essential, to give us a greater treasure.
He is the One who will tenderly refresh the scorched places of our lives.
He is the One who will bring the new green shoots again.
He is the One who nurtures us with His love in the dark place; who brings us into the light with His sweet refreshing rain.
He is the One who pours on us His sunshine; who matures the crop till harvest time when all is made plain; when all can see the fruit.
From scorching fire to harvest time. This is the work of God in our lives.

Shekinah . October 2004.
Madrid.

On a visit to Spain, to celebrate the founding of a new Church in Madrid, we were taken to a Retreat Centre, overlooking a valley which had been devastated by fire. This was the word which came to me then.

Something heard...

Look at your world and understand what I am doing. I am sending a shuddering into your world. I am shaking every structure that is familiar to you. I am testing the fabric and material of society in order to see what will stand.

Those things which are of true value will be worthless. The things which are truly precious will fall unnoticed into the gutter and be trampled under foot.

Truth, justice and faithfulness will become flowers more rare than the wild orchid.

I am shaking the world in my wrath and judgement but do not be terrified, for there is a place of safety for you. It is with Me. I will shelter you under my garments. I will protect you with my strong arm, only remain in Me. Stay close to Me. Cling to Me. Search for my face and long for my presence. Feed from my hand.

Do not try to warm yourselves by the familiar fires of religion and tradition for these will be blown away. Do not comfort yourselves around the fires of affluence and plenty for I will snuff these out also.

Seek my presence for with Me there is safety. Walk with Me.

In this shaking, befriend the friendless, share with the hungry, comfort the bereaved, encourage the young and nurture the little ones. Open your hand to the poor. Love your enemies, and forgive those who wrong you. Share the good news of the Gospel of God.

Act out my Word for all to see and I will sustain you as I shake the world.

NB: Although this came to me in March 1993, when I found it again recently, it seemed very pertinent to our times.

Finally

All of life's elixir
Distils into this single drop of sweetness
That I am His and He is mine
Forever
and
Forever.